EDGE
BOOKS

MINI-BEAST WARS

TARANTULA VS TARANTULA HAWK

BY LINDSY O'BRIEN

CLASH OF THE GIANTS

raintree

a Capstone company — publishers for children

Raintree is an imprint of Capstone Global Library Limited, a company incorporated in England and Wales having its registered office at 264 Banbury Road, Oxford, OX2 7DY – Registered company number: 6695582

www.raintree.co.uk
myorders@raintree.co.uk

ISBN 978 1 4747 1084 8
20 19 18 17 16 15
10 9 8 7 6 5 4 3 2 1

British Library Cataloguing in Publication Data
A full catalogue record for this book is available from the British Library.

Editorial Credits
Aaron Sautter, editor; Russell Griesmer, designer; Jo Miller, media researcher;
Katy LaVigne, production specialist

The publisher would like to thank Christiane Weirauch, Professor of Entomology at University of California, Riverside for her help creating this book.

Photo Credits
Alamy: Bob Jensen, 11, (bottom); Dreamstime: Sb Sullivan, 7, (top); Glow Images: ImageBroker RM/Dirk Funhoff, Cover (left), 4, 9 (top); National Geographic Creative: John Cancalosi, 7 (bottom), 21; Newscom: Custom Medical Stock Photo/Educational Images LTD, 15 (bottom), 22, Custom Medical Stock Photo/John Reid, 13 (top), ImageBROKER/Thomas Vinke, 11 (top), Minden Pictures/Mark Moffett, 25, 27, Photoshot/NHPA/James Carmichael, 15 (top), Reuters/Henry Romero, 13 (bottom), Universal Images Group/Dorling Kindersley, 17; Science Source: Kenneth M. Highfill, 23; Shutterstock: Agustin Esmoris, Cover (right and back), 5, 9 (bottom), 20; SuperStock: Exactostock-1598/Robert Oelman, 29; Wikimedia: Astrobradley, 19

Design Elements
Capstone and Shutterstock

Every effort has been made to cont[...] book. Any omissions will be rectified in s[...]

All the Internet addresses (URLs) g[...]ess. However, due to the dynamic natu[...] or sites may have changed or ceased t[...]ner regret any inconvenience this may [...] can be accepted by either the autho[...]

CONTENTS

WELCOME TO MINI-BEAST WARS!

Whether you see them or not, mini-beast wars are raging around you every day. **Predators** and **prey** fight one another for survival. Insects fight for places to live, to **reproduce** and to protect their young. These battles are often intense. Keep your eyes peeled – you may see one war happening near you!

predator animal that hunts other animals for food

prey animal hunted by another animal for food

reproduce breed and have offspring

In this mini-beast war a tarantula and a tarantula hawk battle it out. First you'll learn about their deadly weapons and how they fight. Then you'll get to see these two huge enemies engage in mortal combat. Which of these massive mini-beasts will win this battle to the death? Settle down and get ready for some wild insect action!

THE COMBATANTS

Many people fear tarantulas and tarantula hawks. That's not surprising. Both of them are big and look scary. Tarantulas are huge, hairy spiders with big fangs. Tarantula hawks are giant wasps with nasty stingers. Tarantula hawks belong to a group of wasps that hunt spiders – especially tarantulas. Both of these huge mini-beasts are fierce towards other insects. But neither tarantulas nor tarantula hawks are aggressive towards humans unless they feel threatened.

Different species of tarantula and tarantula hawk are found on every continent except Antarctica. However, they usually prefer warm climates. They often live in deserts and rainforests around the world.

species group of plants or animals that share common characteristics

SIZE AND WEIGHT

Tarantulas are huge spiders. Most have leg spans of about 13 centimetres (5 inches). That's about as big as an adult's hand. However, the Goliath bird-eating tarantula can grow up to 30.5 cm (1 foot) long! Although tarantulas are large, they aren't very heavy. Most weigh only 28 to 85 grams (1 to 3 ounces).

Tarantula hawks are smaller than tarantulas – but they're still one of the world's biggest insects. North American tarantula hawks can have 7.6-cm (3-in) wingspans. The largest tarantula hawks live in the rainforests of South America. These wasps can have wingspans of up to 11.6 cm (4.5 in) wide. In flight, these huge insects may look like small birds.

FIERCE FACT

THE TARANTULA HAWK WAS VOTED THE STATE INSECT OF NEW MEXICO, USA IN 1989.

RATING ☐☐☐☐☐☐ 5

TARANTULA:
huge hunter

RATING ☐☐☐☐☐☐ 4

TARANTULA HAWK:
giant flyer

MOVEMENT AND STRENGTH

Tarantulas have two or three retractable claws at the end of their legs. When not in use these claws can be pulled in like a cat's claws. The claws help the big spiders climb on steep or slippery surfaces. Tarantulas usually move slowly and carefully. Sometimes they might sit so still that they appear to be dead. But when hunting, they are able to lunge quickly at prey.

Tarantula hawks make short flights by beating their wings rapidly. They can also be found scampering quickly across the desert sand. These big wasps use both movements as they search for prey.

Tarantula hawks are also very strong. They can drag much larger tarantulas across the ground. Sometimes they can even fly awkwardly with tarantulas gripped in their legs.

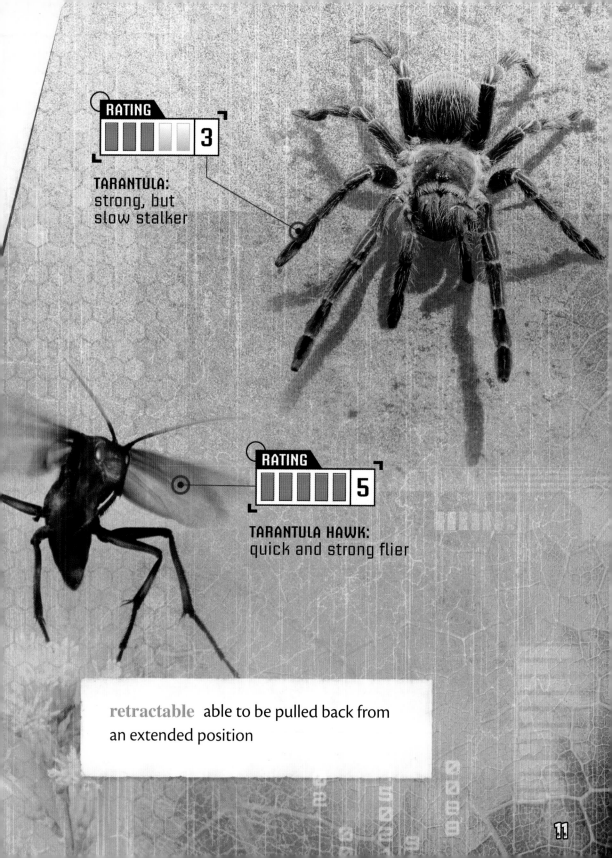

RATING

3

TARANTULA:
strong, but
slow stalker

RATING

5

TARANTULA HAWK:
quick and strong flier

retractable able to be pulled back from
an extended position

DEFENCES

When it comes to defence, the tarantula is very creative. The spider usually hides inside its burrow. It often hides the entrance by covering it with plants or soil. The tarantula may also spin a line of silk outside the burrow entrance. This silk acts like a trip-wire that alerts the spider when prey or enemies approach.

When threatened, the tarantula raises its front legs above its head. People often mistake this as a sign that the tarantula is about to attack. However, this action is meant more as a warning. By making itself look larger, the tarantula hopes that enemies will leave it alone.

Tarantula hawk's defences involve the use of colour and smell. These wasps have bright red wings and metallic blue-black bodies. These bright colours act as a warning and a sign of danger to other animals. The wasps also give off a smell that warns predators about their powerful venom.

burrow hole in the ground made or used by an animal

venom poisonous liquid produced by some animals

FIERCE FACT

MANY TARANTULAS MAKE HISSING SOUNDS AS A WARNING WHEN THEY FEEL THREATENED. THEY DO THIS BY RUBBING TOGETHER TINY BRISTLES FOUND ON THEIR FANGS.

RATING 5

TARANTULA HAWK:
colourful warnings

RATING 2

TARANTULA:
creative defender

WEAPONS

A tarantula's main weapons are its strength, big fangs, and venom. However, tarantula venom is weaker than most types of bee venom. It's only strong enough to paralyse insects and a few small animals. But tarantulas may just crush their prey with their very strong jaws.

Tarantulas are also equipped with special urticating bristles on their abdomens. When they're threatened, the spiders can flick these barbed hairs at enemies to chase them away.

The tarantula hawk's primary weapons are its large stinger and deadly venom. A female's stinger can measure up to 0.8 cm (0.33 in) long. Its venom can paralyse victims in a matter of seconds. The tarantula hawk can also use its strong legs and hooked claws to grapple with its prey. The ability to fly also gives the tarantula hawk a big advantage during a fight.

paralyse loss of the ability to control the muscles

urticate cause painful itching or irritation

RATING

5

TARANTULA:
big poisonous fangs,
strong jaws

FIERCE FACT

ACCORDING TO THE SCHMIDT STING PAIN INDEX, TARANTULA HAWKS HAVE THE SECOND MOST PAINFUL STING IN THE WORLD. THEIR VENOM ISN'T DEADLY TO HUMANS. BUT IT'S POWERFUL ENOUGH TO CAUSE AN ADULT TO FALL TO THE GROUND SCREAMING IN PAIN.

RATING

3

TARANTULA HAWK:
large stinger,
hooked claws

TARANTULA ATTACK STYLE

The tarantula is a sneaky and patient hunter. It normally hides in its burrow and waits for prey to pass by. The spider then lunges from the burrow entrance to ambush its prey. Once outside the tarantula grabs its victim with its strong legs and holds it down. The spider holds its prey long enough to inject venom with its fangs. After the prey is dead, the spider's fangs produce digestive **enzymes** that liquify the victim's insides. The tarantula can then suck up the soupy meal through its straw-like mouthparts.

FIERCE FACT

TARANTULAS USUALLY EAT INSECTS SUCH AS CRICKETS, GRASSHOPPERS AND BEETLES. BUT THEY ARE ALSO KNOWN TO EAT MICE, LIZARDS AND FROGS.

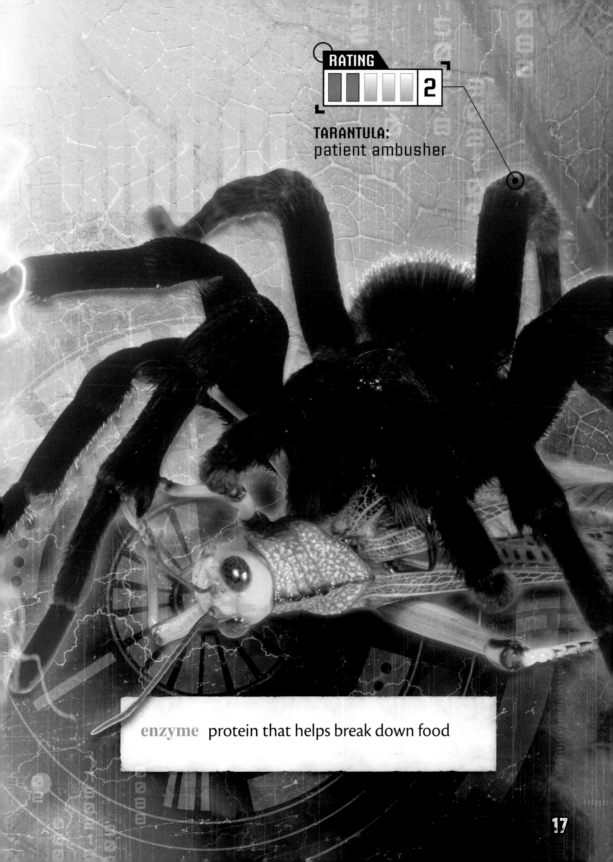

TARANTULA:
patient ambusher

enzyme protein that helps break down food

TARANTULA HAWK ATTACK STYLE

Tarantula hawks use their sense of smell to hunt for and find tarantula burrows. When attacking, some tarantula hawks just sting their prey wherever they can. But the big wasps will often try to push tarantulas over to sting them on their soft stomachs.

Once stung the tarantula becomes paralysed. The tarantula hawk sometimes drags its victim back to its burrow. This can be more than 91 metres (300 ft) away. But the wasp will often use the spider's own burrow instead. The wasp then lays one egg on the tarantula. After the egg hatches, the larva starts to eat the tarantula alive. The tarantula won't die until the larva eats an important organ. The larva avoids doing this to keep the tarantula alive as long as possible. The whole process can take up to 32 days.

FIERCE FACT

ADULT TARANTULA HAWKS DON'T ACTUALLY EAT SPIDERS. THEY USUALLY DRINK NECTAR FROM FLOWERS INSTEAD. HOWEVER, THEY SOMETIMES LIKE TO EAT SWEET FERMENTED FRUIT.

TARANTULA HAWK:
fierce attacker

larva insect at the stage of development between an egg and an adult

ferment undergo a chemical change that turns sugar into alcohol

GET READY TO RUMBLE!

Coming up – a mini-beast war that's sure to be intense! The tarantula is on full alert. Will that be enough when the deadly tarantula hawk comes looking for him? The tarantula is bigger, stronger and has dangerous fangs. But the tarantula hawk has the advantages of speed and her powerful, paralysing venom. Less than 1 in 100 tarantulas survive in battle against tarantula hawks. Will our spider be one of the lucky ones? Get ready for an awesome mini-beast battle!

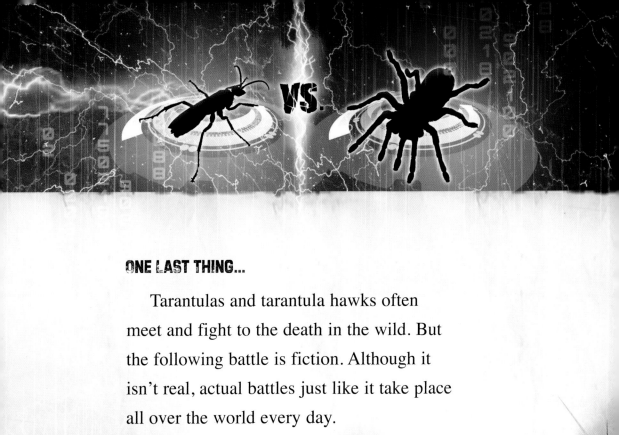

ONE LAST THING...

Tarantulas and tarantula hawks often meet and fight to the death in the wild. But the following battle is fiction. Although it isn't real, actual battles just like it take place all over the world every day.

THE BATTLE BEGINS!

A tarantula sleeps in its desert burrow. His stomach is full from the crickets he ate last night. After his feast, the spider plugged his burrow's entrance with webbing and dead leaves. He also ran a string of silk in front of the entrance. If more tasty insects wander by, he'll know when they hit his trip-wire. However, another dangerous hunter is prowling near by.

FIERCE FACT

OTHER THAN TARANTULA HAWKS, TARANTULAS HAVE FEW NATURAL ENEMIES. ROADRUNNERS AND BULLFROGS SOMETIMES EAT TARANTULAS. SCORPIONS MAY ALSO OVERCOME TARANTULAS WITH THEIR POWERFUL VENOM AND CLAWS.

Outside, a tarantula hawk runs across the sand. The sun gleams off her shiny blue-black body and red wings. She darts and sniffs while seeking out her prey's hiding place. Suddenly she stops. She can smell the tarantula's burrow. Then she sees a glint of sunlight on a thin thread of webbing. It's the spider's trip-wire. She steps up to the silk thread and taps it with her leg.

Below ground, the tarantula wakes. *Prey*, he thinks. He makes his way through the tunnel and gets into position. He pushes open the plug to peek outside. If he sees another juicy cricket, he'll lunge and pounce on it. He waits at his burrow entrance. He can almost taste his next meal.

CLOSE CALLS

But suddenly the tarantula's burrow is filled with sunlight. The tarantula hawk has ripped away the entrance plug. The tarantula is surprised and scared. He raises up his legs to warn his enemy. The big wasp backs off. She drops the plug and beats her wings to lift herself into the air.

Before she gets far, the tarantula lunges at her! But the cunning wasp is too quick. She darts just out of the spider's reach. The tarantula stands up tall with his legs raised. The tarantula hawk sees her chance. She swoops and slams into him, knocking him off balance. The big spider falls backwards and lays sprawled on his back.

FIERCE FACT

TARANTULAS OFTEN LOSE LEGS IN BATTLE. BUT THEY CAN REGROW LOST LEGS WHEN THEY MOLT.

The tarantula flails his legs. He's desperate to flip back onto his feet. The tarantula hawk gets into position and dives for her prey's stomach. But the tarantula is faster. He twists hard and lands on his eight hairy legs.

The big wasp dives for the tarantula again, but he's ready this time. He leaps at her and grabs her with his legs. Tiny barbed bristles shoot from his belly and into his enemy. The wasp's wings crunch as the tarantula squeezes her body. She's been caught.

THE STRIKE

But the battle isn't over. The hawk twists in the tarantula's grip. She slashes at the spider with the hooked claw on her free leg. The tarantula's hold loosens. Suddenly the fierce hunter gives one last powerful push and beats her wings hard. The hawk finally twists out of the spider's grasp. As she breaks free, the tarantula loses its balance. Once again he falls backwards onto the ground – exposing his soft stomach.

The tarantula hawk doesn't wait this time. Before her prey can flip himself over, she plunges her stinger into his soft belly.

Within seconds, the tarantula freezes in place. One leg is still raised above his head. To make sure the spider can't move, the hunter stings her prey again. Then she lands a few centimetres away and waits. Finally she knows that the tarantula is paralysed. She's won this fight.

The tarantula hawk then hooks the tarantula with her curved claws. She drags the spider back to his burrow. A moment later, both mini-beasts disappear underground.

THE AFTERMATH

Deep in the dark burrow, the tarantula hawk lays one egg onto the tarantula's stomach. This spider is large, so she fertilizes the egg. She then flies off in search of another tarantula to battle.

Back in the burrow, the egg hatches into a larva that looks like a white grub. It first eats a hole into the tarantula's stomach. Then it works its way into the spider's body. To keep its food source alive, it avoids eating important organs like the heart or lungs. This gives the larva a fresh store of food as it grows. When the larva does eat one of the vital organs, the spider finally dies.

When it's grown large enough, the larva forms a cocoon. Inside the cocoon it transforms into a female tarantula hawk. When it emerges, the new tarantula hawk will begin its own deadly hunt for tarantulas.

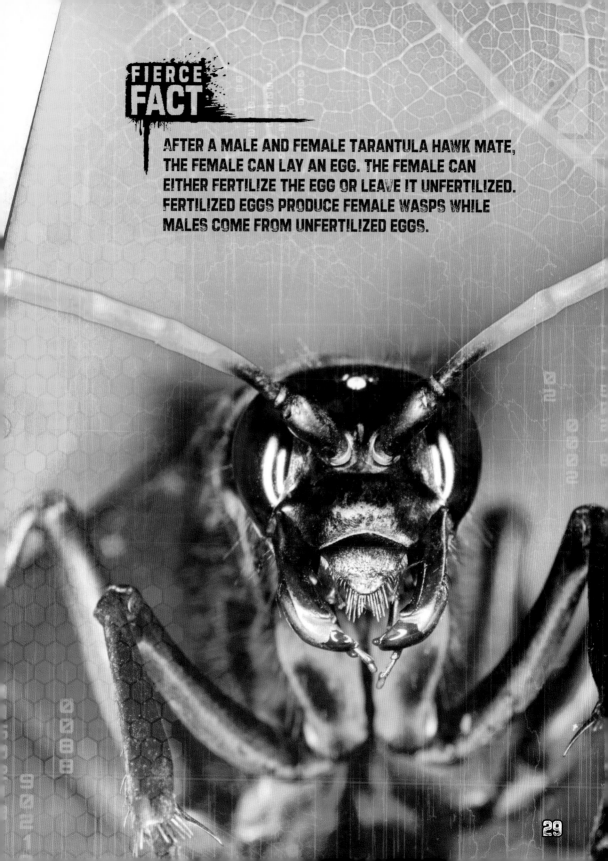

AFTER A MALE AND FEMALE TARANTULA HAWK MATE, THE FEMALE CAN LAY AN EGG. THE FEMALE CAN EITHER FERTILIZE THE EGG OR LEAVE IT UNFERTILIZED. FERTILIZED EGGS PRODUCE FEMALE WASPS WHILE MALES COME FROM UNFERTILIZED EGGS.

GLOSSARY

burrow hole in the ground made or used by an animal

enzyme protein that helps break down food

ferment undergo a chemical change that turns sugar into alcohol

larva insect at the stage of development between an egg and an adult

paralyse loss of the ability to control the muscles

predator animal that hunts other animals for food

prey animal hunted by another animal for food

reproduce breed and have offspring

retractable able to be pulled back from an extended position

species group of plants or animals that share common characteristics

urticate cause painful itching or irritation

venom poisonous liquid produced by some animals

READ MORE

Crazy Creepy Crawlies (Extreme Animals),
Isabel Thomas (Raintree, 2013)

Super Spiders (Walk on the Wild Side),
Charlotte Guillain (Raintree, 2014)

Tarantula vs Bird (Predator vs Prey),
Mary Meinking Chambers (Raintree, 2012)

WEBSITES

**www.animalplanet.com/tv-shows/the-most-extreme/
videos/tarantula-vs-tarantula-hawk/**
View a video of a tarantula and a tarantula hawk in a battle
to the death.

www.britannica.com/animal/tarantula
Find out more about various species of tarantulas, their
features and their behaviours.

www.desertusa.com/insects/tarantula-hawks.html
Learn more about the features and behaviours of tarantula
hawks, and view a video of one of these giant wasps in action.

INDEX